Metamorphosis

An Annual Record of Transformation

Created By
Rebecca Marklund

Metamorphosis
Copyright © 2022 by Rebecca Marklund

tellwell

Tellwell Talent
www.tellwell.ca

ISBN
978-0-2288-7618-2 (Hardcover)
978-0-2288-7617-5 (Paperback)

Metamorphosis

An Annual record of Transformation

by Rebecca Marklund

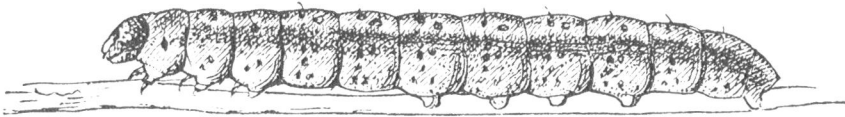

WELCOME BRAVE SOULS,

Webster's dictionary defines metamorphosis as a "change of physical form, structure, or substance especially by supernatural means"

We are all on a journey of discovery from the moment take our first breath, to the time we take our last here on earth. Some of the changes are kind and gentle, and others harsh and excruciatingly painful. Some are welcomed, others come as thieves in the night.

This annual day timer and journal allows for tracking relevant information in this transformation process, with Proverbs and quotes to encourage growth in wisdom, discernment, purpose and reflection.

It's my hope and prayer that you press into your process with bravery and courage as you transform into the best version of yourself. Allow time to name and process the feelings that come with the process of growth. Be kind with the process with yourself. Be kind with the process in others.
And be brave dear ones....
Be brave.

Rebecca

METAMORPHOSIS

Gratitude - Since my children were little, I've always had a gratitude journal on an antique hutch in our home. Daily, it's become our practice to take time and reflect and record the blessings that perhaps would go unnoticed or overshadowed by the louder events in our day. I truly believe there is always something to be grateful for if we are choosing to look for these gifts regularly. The practice of gratitude has often been what has sustained us through difficult seasons. Today, these journals of gratitude from years past are some of our most cherished possessions. The practice of gratitude one of our most valuable life altering habits we have developed over the years.

Truths - During the many seasons of life, it is important to remember truths that will keep us on our course. Writing these truths down is grounding and emotionally stabilizing when often our world's can be upside down. Reflection and review of these things that remain consistent is grounding, as life is constantly transitioning and changing. Our mind isn't always telling us the truth, and we need to constantly reorientate ourselves in seasons of uncertainty to remain grounded.

Challenges - This section is for a record of the daily challenges we face. There is something powerful about writing it down, and getting it out of our heads and hearts and onto paper. Writing it down takes it from the inside out, brings it to light and gives us the ability to look and process it more objectively. I believe it also lessens the power it has to affect us physiologically when we get it out, rather then let it ruminate on the inside.

METAMORPHOSIS

Encounters and Feelings - It is beneficial we recognize and develop vocabulary and proper association of feelings with encounters we face daily. In the practice of identifying events, and attaching associated feelings to the event, it creates greater emotional intelligence and broader understanding and language of the many variety of feelings we may encounter

Self care/Soul Care - This is a space to record the practices that are beneficial to strengthen yourself, and your soul. Practices might include journaling, prayer, meditation, exercise, time with friends and loved ones, learning, hobbies or creative outlets (this list is not extensive by any means.) It is vital to take time to refuel on a routine basis, in order to maintain the capacity for the tasks which are required of you.

Lies I need to replace - There is a constant battle in our minds of lies and truth. These lies may have come from childhood, culture, or a faulty belief system we adopted somewhere along the way. The seeds of our beliefs bring forth actions in our lives. When we are conscious of a faulty thought pattern, it is important to recognize it, name it as falsehood, and replace it with a truth. In practicing this, we retrain our brain to believe the truths rather than lies.

Feelings List

Identify the event, then the feeling associated with it.
Name it, own it, but don't let it steer your ship.

stressed
overwhelmed
anxious
worried
avoidance
excitement
fear
vulnerability
comparison
admiration
reverence
envy
jealousy
resentment
boredom
disappointment
regret
discouragment
resignation
frustration
awe
wonder
confustion
curiosity
interest
surprise
amusement
bittersweetness

hopelessness
hopefullness
sadness
grief
compassion
pity
empathy
sympathy
vulnerable
shame
perfectionism
guilt
comparison
humiliation
embarrasment
belonging
connection
disconnection
insecurity
invisiblity
invalidation
loneliness
love
heartbreak
trust
betrayal
defensiveness

flooding
hurt
joy
happiness
calm
contentment
Gratitude
relief
tranquility
anger
contempt
disgust
hate
peace
nostalgia
paradox
sarcasm
anguish

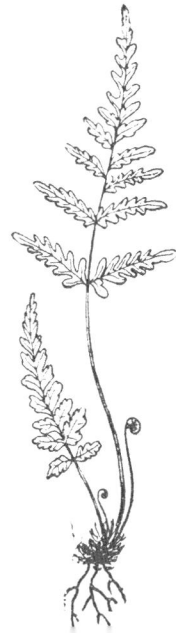

GOALS FOR GROWTH

JANUARY

S	M	T	W	T	F	S

WEEKLY PLANNER

week of: _____

MONDAY

TUESDAY

WEDNESDAY

THURSDAY

FRIDAY

SATURDAY

SUNDAY

METAMORPHOSIS

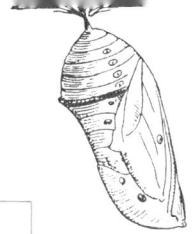

week of: _____

GRATITUDE

TRUTHS

CHALLENGES

ENCOUNTERS AND FEELINGS

SELF CARE/SOUL CARE

LIES I NEED TO REPLACE

NOTES

"The secret to living gloriously is to live imperfectly with great delight."
Unknown

WEEKLY PLANNER

week of: _____

MONDAY

TUESDAY

WEDNESDAY

THURSDAY

FRIDAY

SATURDAY

SUNDAY

METAMORPHOSIS

week of: _____

GRATITUDE

TRUTHS

OPPORTUNITIES FOR GROWTH

ENCOUNTERS AND FEELINGS

SELF CARE/SOUL CARE

LIES I NEED TO REPLACE

NOTES

"I will forsake unforgiveness for the sake of Shalom in my soul."
Unknown

WEEKLY PLANNER

week of: _____

MONDAY

TUESDAY

WEDNESDAY

THURSDAY

FRIDAY

SATURDAY

SUNDAY

METAMORPHOSIS

week of: _____

GRATITUDE

TRUTHS

OPPORTUNITIES FOR GROWTH

ENCOUNTERS AND FEELINGS

SELF CARE/SOUL CARE

LIES I NEED TO REPLACE

NOTES

"Success is not final. Failure is not fatal.
It is the courage to continue that counts."
Winston Churchill

WEEKLY PLANNER

week of: _____

MONDAY

TUESDAY

WEDNESDAY

THURSDAY

FRIDAY

SATURDAY

SUNDAY

METAMORPHOSIS

week of: _____

GRATITUDE

TRUTHS

OPPORTUNITIES FOR GROWTH

ENCOUNTERS AND FEELINGS

SELF CARE/SOUL CARE

LIES I NEED TO REPLACE

NOTES

"Let love and faithfulness never leave you; bind them around your neck,
write them on the tablet of your heart"
Proverbs 3:3

WEEKLY PLANNER

week of: _____

MONDAY

TUESDAY

WEDNESDAY

THURSDAY

FRIDAY

SATURDAY

SUNDAY

METAMORPHOSIS

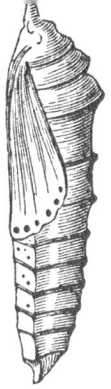

week of: _____

GRATITUDE

TRUTHS

OPPORTUNITIES FOR GROWTH

ENCOUNTERS AND FEELINGS

SELF CARE/SOUL CARE

LIES I NEED TO REPLACE

NOTES

"In a world that never stops, give yourself permission to rest. It's ok to rest."
Rebecca Marklund

FEBRUARY

S	M	T	W	T	F	S

WEEKLY PLANNER

week of: _____

MONDAY

TUESDAY

WEDNESDAY

THURSDAY

FRIDAY

SATURDAY

SUNDAY

METAMORPHOSIS

week of: _____

GRATITUDE

TRUTHS

OPPORTUNITIES FOR GROWTH

ENCOUNTERS AND FEELINGS

SELF CARE/SOUL CARE

LIES I NEED TO REPLACE

NOTES

"Blessed is the man who finds wisdom, the man who gains understanding,
for she is more profitable than silver, and yields better returns than gold."
Proverbs 3: 13 & 14

WEEKLY PLANNER

week of: _____

MONDAY

TUESDAY

WEDNESDAY

THURSDAY

FRIDAY

SATURDAY

SUNDAY

METAMORPHOSIS

week of: _____

GRATITUDE

TRUTHS

OPPORTUNITIES FOR GROWTH

ENCOUNTERS AND FEELINGS

SELF CARE/SOUL CARE

LIES I NEED TO REPLACE

NOTES

"My son, preserve sound judgment and discernment, do not let them out of your sight; they will be
life to you, and ornament to grace your neck."
Proverbs 3: 21 & 22

WEEKLY PLANNER

week of: _____

MONDAY

TUESDAY

WEDNESDAY

THURSDAY

FRIDAY

SATURDAY

SUNDAY

METAMORPHOSIS

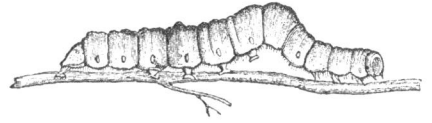

week of: _____

GRATITUDE

TRUTHS

OPPORTUNITIES FOR GROWTH

ENCOUNTERS AND FEELINGS

SELF CARE/SOUL CARE

LIES I NEED TO REPLACE

NOTES

"You're a diamond dear. They can't break you."
Unknown

WEEKLY PLANNER

week of: _____

MONDAY

TUESDAY

WEDNESDAY

THURSDAY

FRIDAY

SATURDAY

SUNDAY

METAMORPHOSIS

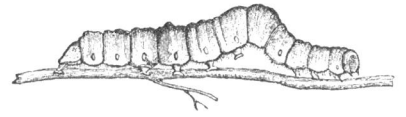

week of: _____

GRATITUDE

TRUTHS

OPPORTUNITIES FOR GROWTH

ENCOUNTERS AND FEELINGS

SELF CARE/SOUL CARE

LIES I NEED TO REPLACE

NOTES

"Tell me and I forget. Teach me and I remember. Involve me and I learn."
Benjamin Franklin

NOTES AND REFLECTION

MARCH

S	M	T	W	T	F	S

WEEKLY PLANNER

week of: _____

MONDAY

TUESDAY

WEDNESDAY

THURSDAY

FRIDAY

SATURDAY

SUNDAY

METAMORPHOSIS

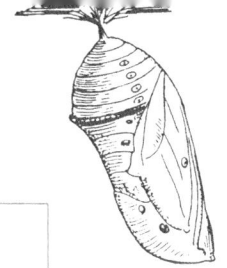

week of: _____

GRATITUDE

TRUTHS

OPPORTUNITIES FOR GROWTH

ENCOUNTERS AND FEELINGS

SELF CARE/SOUL CARE

LIES I NEED TO REPLACE

NOTES

"Do not withhold good from those who deserve it,
when it is in your power to act"
Proverbs 3:27

WEEKLY PLANNER

week of: _____

MONDAY

TUESDAY

WEDNESDAY

THURSDAY

FRIDAY

SATURDAY

SUNDAY

METAMORPHOSIS

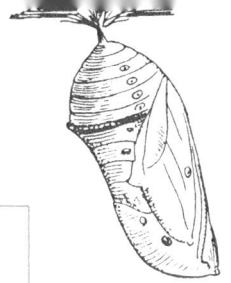

week of: _____

GRATITUDE

TRUTHS

OPPORTUNITIES FOR GROWTH

ENCOUNTERS AND FEELINGS

SELF CARE/SOUL CARE

LIES I NEED TO REPLACE

NOTES

"Sometimes memories sneak out of my eyes and roll down my cheeks."
Unknown

WEEKLY PLANNER

week of: _____

MONDAY

TUESDAY

WEDNESDAY

THURSDAY

FRIDAY

SATURDAY

SUNDAY

METAMORPHOSIS

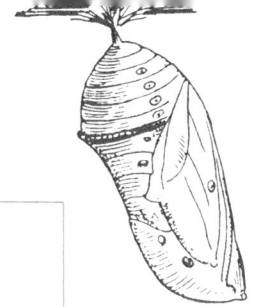

week of: _____

GRATITUDE

TRUTHS

OPPORTUNITIES FOR GROWTH

ENCOUNTERS AND FEELINGS

SELF CARE/SOUL CARE

LIES I NEED TO REPLACE

NOTES

"It is during our darkest moments that we must focus to see the light."
Aristotle

WEEKLY PLANNER

week of: _____

MONDAY

TUESDAY

WEDNESDAY

THURSDAY

FRIDAY

SATURDAY

SUNDAY

METAMORPHOSIS

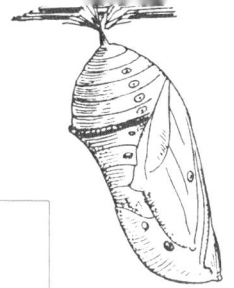

week of: _____

GRATITUDE

TRUTHS

OPPORTUNITIES FOR GROWTH

ENCOUNTERS AND FEELINGS

SELF CARE /SOUL CARE

LIES I NEED TO REPLACE

NOTES

"Do not forsake wisdom, and she will protect you;
love her, and she will watch over you"
Proverbs 4:6

NOTES AND REFLECTION

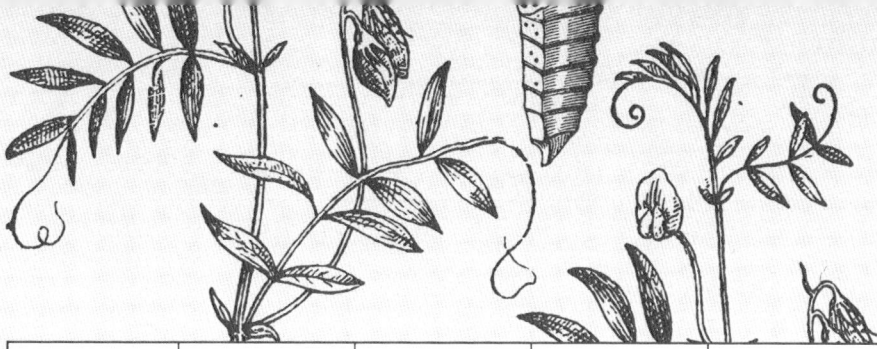

APRIL

S	M	T	W	T	F	S

WEEKLY PLANNER

week of: _____

MONDAY

TUESDAY

WEDNESDAY

THURSDAY

FRIDAY

SATURDAY

SUNDAY

METAMORPHOSIS

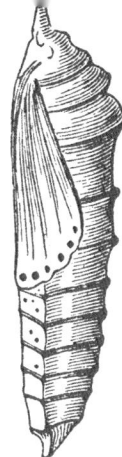

week of: _____

GRATITUDE

TRUTHS

OPPORTUNITIES FOR GROWTH

ENCOUNTERS AND FEELINGS

SELF CARE/SOUL CARE

LIES I NEED TO REPLACE

NOTES

"Whoever is happy will make others happy too."
Anne Frank

WEEKLY PLANNER

week of: _____

MONDAY

TUESDAY

WEDNESDAY

THURSDAY

FRIDAY

SATURDAY

SUNDAY

METAMORPHOSIS

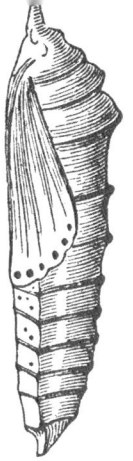

week of: _____

GRATITUDE

TRUTHS

OPPORTUNITIES FOR GROWTH

ENCOUNTERS AND FEELINGS

SELF CARE/SOUL CARE

LIES I NEED TO REPLACE

NOTES

"Wisdom is supreme; therefore get wisdom.
Though it cost all you have, get understanding."
Proverbs 4:7

WEEKLY PLANNER

week of: _____

MONDAY

TUESDAY

WEDNESDAY

THURSDAY

FRIDAY

SATURDAY

SUNDAY

METAMORPHOSIS

week of: _____

GRATITUDE

TRUTHS

OPPORTUNITIES FOR GROWTH

ENCOUNTERS AND FEELINGS

SELF CARE/SOUL CARE

LIES I NEED TO REPLACE

NOTES

"Do not go where the path may lead,
go instead where there is no path and leave a trail."
Ralph Waldo Emerson

WEEKLY PLANNER

week of: _____

MONDAY

TUESDAY

WEDNESDAY

THURSDAY

FRIDAY

SATURDAY

SUNDAY

METAMORPHOSIS

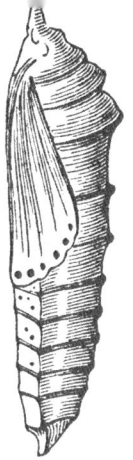

week of: _____

GRATITUDE

TRUTHS

OPPORTUNITIES FOR GROWTH

ENCOUNTERS AND FEELINGS

SELF CARE/SOUL CARE

LIES I NEED TO REPLACE

NOTES

"Above all else, guard your heart, for it is the wellspring of life."
Proverbs 4:23

NOTES AND REFLECTION

MAY

S	M	T	W	T	F	S

WEEKLY PLANNER

week of: _____

MONDAY

TUESDAY

WEDNESDAY

THURSDAY

FRIDAY

SATURDAY

SUNDAY

METAMORPHOSIS

week of: _____

GRATITUDE

TRUTHS

OPPORTUNITIES FOR GROWTH

ENCOUNTERS AND FEELINGS

SELF CARE/SOUL CARE

LIES I NEED TO REPLACE

NOTES

"When you reach the end of your rope, tie a knot in it and hang on."
Franklin D. Roosevelt

WEEKLY PLANNER

week of: _____

MONDAY

TUESDAY

WEDNESDAY

THURSDAY

FRIDAY

SATURDAY

SUNDAY

METAMORPHOSIS

week of: _____

GRATITUDE

TRUTHS

OPPORTUNITIES FOR GROWTH

ENCOUNTERS AND FEELINGS

SELF CARE/SOUL CARE

LIES I NEED TO REPLACE

NOTES

"Let your eyes look straight ahead, fix your gaze directly before you.
Make level paths for your feet and take only ways that are firm."
Proverbs 4:26

WEEKLY PLANNER

week of: _____

MONDAY

TUESDAY

WEDNESDAY

THURSDAY

FRIDAY

SATURDAY

SUNDAY

METAMORPHOSIS

week of: _____

GRATITUDE

TRUTHS

OPPORTUNITIES FOR GROWTH

ENCOUNTERS AND FEELINGS

SELF CARE/SOUL CARE

LIES I NEED TO REPLACE

NOTES

"Don't judge each day by the harvest you reap
but by the seeds that you plant."
Robert Louis Stevenson

WEEKLY PLANNER

week of: _____

MONDAY

TUESDAY

WEDNESDAY

THURSDAY

FRIDAY

SATURDAY

SUNDAY

METAMORPHOSIS

week of: _____

GRATITUDE

TRUTHS

OPPORTUNITIES FOR GROWTH

ENCOUNTERS AND FEELINGS

SELF CARE/SOUL CARE

LIES I NEED TO REPLACE

NOTES

"You who are simple, gain prudence;
you who are foolish, gain understanding."
Proverbs 8:5

WEEKLY PLANNER

week of: _____

MONDAY

TUESDAY

WEDNESDAY

THURSDAY

FRIDAY

SATURDAY

SUNDAY

METAMORPHOSIS

week of: _____

GRATITUDE

TRUTHS

OPPORTUNITIES FOR GROWTH

ENCOUNTERS AND FEELINGS

SELF CARE/SOUL CARE

LIES I NEED TO REPLACE

NOTES

"Grieve the dream, embrace the reality."
Rebecca Marklund

JUNE

S	M	T	W	T	F	S

WEEKLY PLANNER

week of: _____

MONDAY

TUESDAY

WEDNESDAY

THURSDAY

FRIDAY

SATURDAY

SUNDAY

METAMORPHOSIS

week of: _____

GRATITUDE

TRUTHS

OPPORTUNITIES FOR GROWTH

ENCOUNTERS AND FEELINGS

SELF CARE/SOUL CARE

LIES I NEED TO REPLACE

NOTES

"I wisdom, dwell together with prudence;
I possess knowledge and discretion."
Proverbs 8: 12

WEEKLY PLANNER

week of: _____

MONDAY

TUESDAY

WEDNESDAY

THURSDAY

FRIDAY

SATURDAY

SUNDAY

METAMORPHOSIS

week of: _____

GRATITUDE

TRUTHS

OPPORTUNITIES FOR GROWTH

ENCOUNTERS AND FEELINGS

SELF CARE/SOUL CARE

LIES I NEED TO REPLACE

NOTES

"The future belongs to those who believe in the beauty of their dreams."
Eleanor Roosevelt

WEEKLY PLANNER

week of: _____

MONDAY

TUESDAY

WEDNESDAY

THURSDAY

FRIDAY

SATURDAY

SUNDAY

METAMORPHOSIS

week of: _____

GRATITUDE

TRUTHS

OPPORTUNITIES FOR GROWTH

ENCOUNTERS AND FEELINGS

SELF CARE/SOUL CARE

LIES I NEED TO REPLACE

NOTES

"Do not rebuke a mocker or he will hate you;
rebuke a wise man and he will love you."
Proverbs 9:8

WEEKLY PLANNER

week of: _____

MONDAY

TUESDAY

WEDNESDAY

THURSDAY

FRIDAY

SATURDAY

SUNDAY

METAMORPHOSIS

week of: _____

GRATITUDE

TRUTHS

OPPORTUNITIES FOR GROWTH

ENCOUNTERS AND FEELINGS

SELF CARE/SOUL CARE

LIES I NEED TO REPLACE

NOTES

"The greatest glory in living lies not in never falling, but in rising every time we fall."
Nelson Mandela

NOTES AND REFLECTION

JULY

S	M	T	W	T	F	S

WEEKLY PLANNER

week of: _____

MONDAY

TUESDAY

WEDNESDAY

THURSDAY

FRIDAY

SATURDAY

SUNDAY

METAMORPHOSIS

week of: _____

GRATITUDE

TRUTHS

OPPORTUNITIES FOR GROWTH

ENCOUNTERS AND FEELINGS

SELF CARE/SOUL CARE

LIES I NEED TO REPLACE

NOTES

"Lazy hands make a man poor, but diligent hands bring wealth."
Proverbs 10:4

WEEKLY PLANNER

week of: _____

MONDAY

TUESDAY

WEDNESDAY

THURSDAY

FRIDAY

SATURDAY

SUNDAY

METAMORPHOSIS

week of: _____

GRATITUDE

TRUTHS

OPPORTUNITIES FOR GROWTH

ENCOUNTERS AND FEELINGS

SELF CARE/SOUL CARE

LIES I NEED TO REPLACE

NOTES

"In the end, it's not the years in your life that count.
It's the life in your years."
Abraham Lincoln

WEEKLY PLANNER

week of: _____

MONDAY

TUESDAY

WEDNESDAY

THURSDAY

FRIDAY

SATURDAY

SUNDAY

METAMORPHOSIS

week of: _____

GRATITUDE

TRUTHS

OPPORTUNITIES FOR GROWTH

ENCOUNTERS AND FEELINGS

SELF CARE/SOUL CARE

LIES I NEED TO REPLACE

NOTES

"You survived what you thought would kill you. Now straighten your crown and move forward like the queen you are."
Anonymous

WEEKLY PLANNER

week of: _____

MONDAY

TUESDAY

WEDNESDAY

THURSDAY

FRIDAY

SATURDAY

SUNDAY

METAMORPHOSIS

week of: _____

GRATITUDE

TRUTHS

OPPORTUNITIES FOR GROWTH

ENCOUNTERS AND FEELINGS

SELF CARE/SOUL CARE

LIES I NEED TO REPLACE

NOTES

"The wise in heart accept commands,
but a chattering fool comes to ruin."
Proverbs 10:8

WEEKLY PLANNER

week of: _____

MONDAY

TUESDAY

WEDNESDAY

THURSDAY

FRIDAY

SATURDAY

SUNDAY

METAMORPHOSIS

week of: _____

GRATITUDE

TRUTHS

OPPORTUNITIES FOR GROWTH

ENCOUNTERS AND FEELINGS

SELF CARE/SOUL CARE

LIES I NEED TO REPLACE

NOTES

"The man of integrity walks securely,
but he who takes crooked paths will be found out."
Proverbs 10:9

NOTES AND REFLECTION

AUGUST

S	M	T	W	T	F	S

WEEKLY PLANNER

week of: _____

MONDAY

TUESDAY

WEDNESDAY

THURSDAY

FRIDAY

SATURDAY

SUNDAY

METAMORPHOSIS

week of: _____

GRATITUDE

TRUTHS

OPPORTUNITIES FOR GROWTH

ENCOUNTERS AND FEELINGS

SELF CARE/SOUL CARE

LIES I NEED TO REPLACE

NOTES

"He who conceals his hatred has lying lips,
and whoever spreads slander is a fool."
Proverbs 10:18

WEEKLY PLANNER

week of: _____

MONDAY

TUESDAY

WEDNESDAY

THURSDAY

FRIDAY

SATURDAY

SUNDAY

METAMORPHOSIS

week of: _____

GRATITUDE

TRUTHS

OPPORTUNITIES FOR GROWTH

ENCOUNTERS AND FEELINGS

SELF CARE/SOUL CARE

LIES I NEED TO REPLACE

NOTES

Many of life's failures are people who did not realize
how close they were to success when they gave up."
Thomas A. Edison

WEEKLY PLANNER

week of: _____

MONDAY

TUESDAY

WEDNESDAY

THURSDAY

FRIDAY

SATURDAY

SUNDAY

METAMORPHOSIS

week of: _____

GRATITUDE

TRUTHS

OPPORTUNITIES FOR GROWTH

ENCOUNTERS AND FEELINGS

SELF CARE/SOUL CARE

LIES I NEED TO REPLACE

NOTES

"When words are many, sin is not absent,
but he who holds his tongue is wise."
Proverbs 10:19

WEEKLY PLANNER

week of: _____

MONDAY

TUESDAY

WEDNESDAY

THURSDAY

FRIDAY

SATURDAY

SUNDAY

METAMORPHOSIS

week of: _____

GRATITUDE

TRUTHS

OPPORTUNITIES FOR GROWTH

ENCOUNTERS AND FEELINGS

SELF CARE/SOUL CARE

LIES I NEED TO REPLACE

NOTES

"Sometimes fear does not subside. One must do it afraid."
Elisabeth Elliot

WEEKLY PLANNER

week of: _____

MONDAY

TUESDAY

WEDNESDAY

THURSDAY

FRIDAY

SATURDAY

SUNDAY

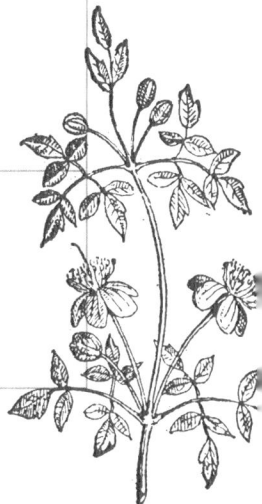

METAMORPHOSIS

week of: _____

GRATITUDE

TRUTHS

OPPORTUNITIES FOR GROWTH

ENCOUNTERS AND FEELINGS

SELF CARE/SOUL CARE

LIES I NEED TO REPLACE

NOTES

"Enough is as good as a feast."
English Proverb

NOTES AND REFLECTION

SEPTEMBER

S	M	T	W	T	F	S

WEEKLY PLANNER

week of: _____

MONDAY

TUESDAY

WEDNESDAY

THURSDAY

FRIDAY

SATURDAY

SUNDAY

METAMORPHOSIS

week of: _____

GRATITUDE

TRUTHS

OPPORTUNITIES FOR GROWTH

ENCOUNTERS AND FEELINGS

SELF CARE/SOUL CARE

LIES I NEED TO REPLACE

NOTES

"The integrity of the upright guides them, but the unfaithful are destroyed by their duplicity"
Proverbs 11:3

WEEKLY PLANNER

week of: _____

MONDAY

TUESDAY

WEDNESDAY

THURSDAY

FRIDAY

SATURDAY

SUNDAY

METAMORPHOSIS

week of: _____

GRATITUDE

TRUTHS

OPPORTUNITIES FOR GROWTH

ENCOUNTERS AND FEELINGS

SELF CARE/SOUL CARE

LIES I NEED TO REPLACE

NOTES

"Life is a succession of lessons which must be lived to be understood."
Ralph Waldo Emerson

WEEKLY PLANNER

week of: _____

MONDAY

TUESDAY

WEDNESDAY

THURSDAY

FRIDAY

SATURDAY

SUNDAY

METAMORPHOSIS

week of: _____

GRATITUDE

TRUTHS

OPPORTUNITIES FOR GROWTH

ENCOUNTERS AND FEELINGS

SELF CARE/SOUL CARE

LIES I NEED TO REPLACE

NOTES

"Making a life change is scary. But you know what's scarier? Regret."
Unknown

WEEKLY PLANNER

week of: _____

MONDAY

TUESDAY

WEDNESDAY

THURSDAY

FRIDAY

SATURDAY

SUNDAY

METAMORPHOSIS

week of: _____

GRATITUDE

TRUTHS

OPPORTUNITIES FOR GROWTH

ENCOUNTERS AND FEELINGS

SELF CARE/SOUL CARE

LIES I NEED TO REPLACE

NOTES

"There will always be people in your life who treat you wrong.
Be sure to thank them for making you strong."
Zig Ziglar

NOTES AND REFLECTION

OCTOBER

S	M	T	W	T	F	S

WEEKLY PLANNER

week of: _____

MONDAY

TUESDAY

WEDNESDAY

THURSDAY

FRIDAY

SATURDAY

SUNDAY

METAMORPHOSIS

week of: _____

GRATITUDE

TRUTHS

OPPORTUNITIES FOR GROWTH

ENCOUNTERS AND FEELINGS

SELF CARE/SOUL CARE

LIES I NEED TO REPLACE

NOTES

"A gossip betrays a confidence, but a trustworthy man keeps a secret."
Proverbs 11: 13

WEEKLY PLANNER

week of: _____

MONDAY

TUESDAY

WEDNESDAY

THURSDAY

FRIDAY

SATURDAY

SUNDAY

METAMORPHOSIS

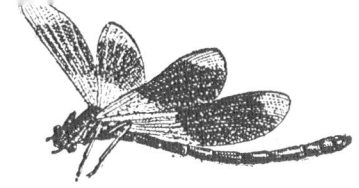

week of: _____

GRATITUDE

TRUTHS

OPPORTUNITIES FOR GROWTH

ENCOUNTERS AND FEELINGS

SELF CARE/SOUL CARE

LIES I NEED TO REPLACE

NOTES

""Life is never fair, and perhaps
it is a good thing for most of us that it is not."
Oscar Wilde

WEEKLY PLANNER

week of: _____

MONDAY

TUESDAY

WEDNESDAY

THURSDAY

FRIDAY

SATURDAY

SUNDAY

METAMORPHOSIS

week of: _____

GRATITUDE

TRUTHS

OPPORTUNITIES FOR GROWTH

ENCOUNTERS AND FEELINGS

SELF CARE/SOUL CARE

LIES I NEED TO REPLACE

NOTES

"For lack of guidance a nation falls,
but many advisors make a victory sure."
Proverbs 11: 14

WEEKLY PLANNER

week of: _____

MONDAY

TUESDAY

WEDNESDAY

THURSDAY

FRIDAY

SATURDAY

SUNDAY

METAMORPHOSIS

GRATITUDE

TRUTHS

OPPORTUNITIES FOR GROWTH

ENCOUNTERS AND FEELINGS

SELF CARE/SOUL CARE

LIES I NEED TO REPLACE

NOTES

"Shoulders back, deep breath, head high, big girl panties on."
Sheila Parry

WEEKLY PLANNER

week of: _____

MONDAY

TUESDAY

WEDNESDAY

THURSDAY

FRIDAY

SATURDAY

SUNDAY

METAMORPHOSIS

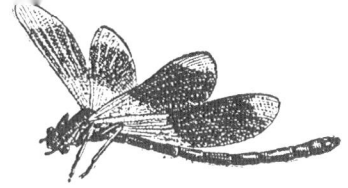

week of: _____

GRATITUDE

TRUTHS

OPPORTUNITIES FOR GROWTH

ENCOUNTERS AND FEELINGS

SELF CARE/SOUL CARE

LIES I NEED TO REPLACE

NOTES

"Today I shall behave, as if this is the day I will be remembered."
Dr Seuss

NOTES AND REFLECTION

NOVEMBER

S	M	T	W	T	F	S

WEEKLY PLANNER

week of: _____

MONDAY

TUESDAY

WEDNESDAY

THURSDAY

FRIDAY

SATURDAY

SUNDAY

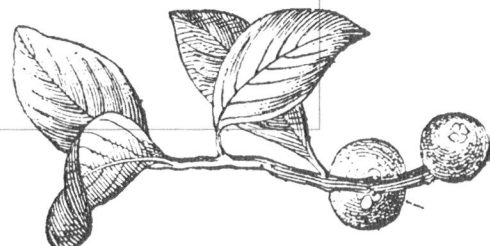

METAMORPHOSIS

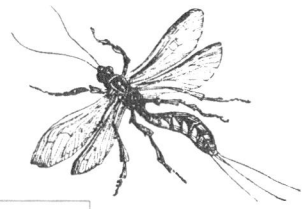

GRATITUDE

TRUTHS

OPPORTUNITIES FOR GROWTH

ENCOUNTERS AND FEELINGS

SELF CARE/SOUL CARE

LIES I NEED TO REPLACE

NOTES

"A kindhearted woman gains respect, but ruthless men gain only wealth."
Proverbs 11:16

WEEKLY PLANNER

week of: _____

MONDAY

TUESDAY

WEDNESDAY

THURSDAY

FRIDAY

SATURDAY

SUNDAY

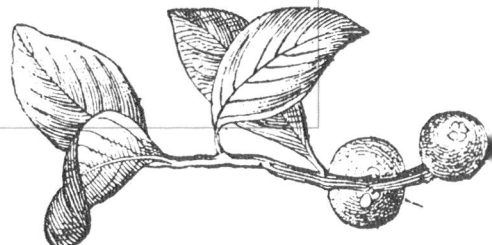

METAMORPHOSIS

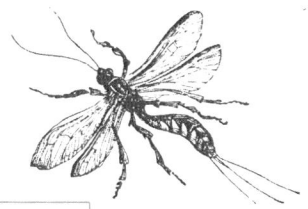

week of: _____

GRATITUDE

TRUTHS

OPPORTUNITIES FOR GROWTH

ENCOUNTERS AND FEELINGS

SELF CARE/SOUL CARE

LIES I NEED TO REPLACE

NOTES

"When we are brave, it inspires others to be brave also."
Rebecca Marklund

WEEKLY PLANNER

week of: _____

MONDAY

TUESDAY

WEDNESDAY

THURSDAY

FRIDAY

SATURDAY

SUNDAY

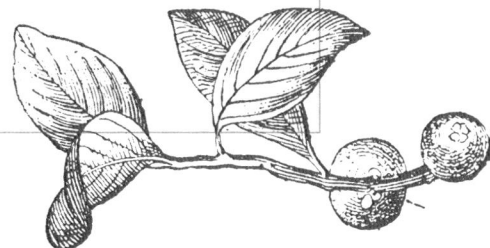

METAMORPHOSIS

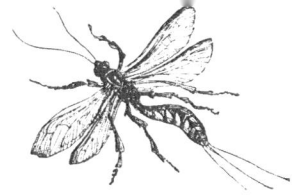

week of: _____

GRATITUDE

TRUTHS

OPPORTUNITIES FOR GROWTH

ENCOUNTERS AND FEELINGS

SELF CARE/SOUL CARE

LIES I NEED TO REPLACE

NOTES

"A kind man benefits himself, but a cruel man brings trouble on himself"
Proverbs 11:17

WEEKLY PLANNER

week of: _____

MONDAY

TUESDAY

WEDNESDAY

THURSDAY

FRIDAY

SATURDAY

SUNDAY

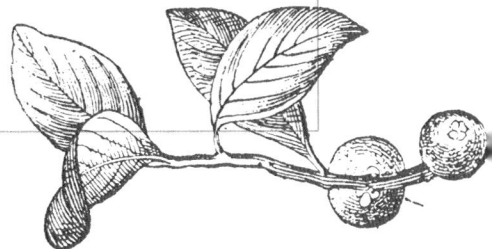

METAMORPHOSIS

week of: _____

GRATITUDE

TRUTHS

OPPORTUNITIES FOR GROWTH

ENCOUNTERS AND FEELINGS

SELF CARE/SOUL CARE

LIES I NEED TO REPLACE

NOTES

"I failed my way to success."
Thomas Edison

WEEKLY PLANNER

week of: _____

MONDAY

TUESDAY

WEDNESDAY

THURSDAY

FRIDAY

SATURDAY

SUNDAY

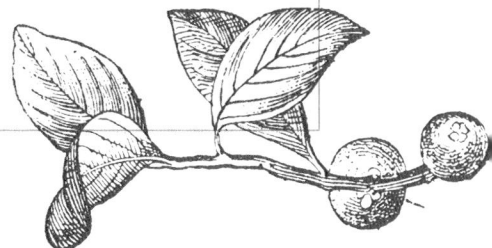

METAMORPHOSIS

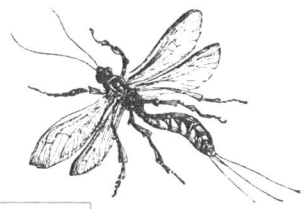

week of: _____

GRATITUDE

TRUTHS

OPPORTUNITIES FOR GROWTH

ENCOUNTERS AND FEELINGS

SELF CARE/SOUL CARE

LIES I NEED TO REPLACE

NOTES

"We have control over our attitudes and perspectives.
May we have wisdom to choose well."
Rebecca Marklund

NOTES AND REFLECTION

DECEMBER

S	M	T	W	T	F	S

WEEKLY PLANNER

week of: _____

MONDAY

TUESDAY

WEDNESDAY

THURSDAY

FRIDAY

SATURDAY

SUNDAY

METAMORPHOSIS

week of: _____

GRATITUDE

TRUTHS

OPPORTUNITIES FOR GROWTH

ENCOUNTERS AND FEELINGS

SELF CARE/SOUL CARE

LIES I NEED TO REPLACE

NOTES

"One man gives freely, yet gains even more;
another withholds unduly, but comes to poverty"
Proverbs 11:24

WEEKLY PLANNER

week of: _____

MONDAY

TUESDAY

WEDNESDAY

THURSDAY

FRIDAY

SATURDAY

SUNDAY

METAMORPHOSIS

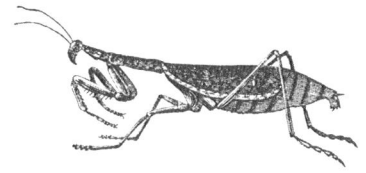

week of: _____

GRATITUDE

TRUTHS

OPPORTUNITIES FOR GROWTH

ENCOUNTERS AND FEELINGS

SELF CARE/SOUL CARE

LIES I NEED TO REPLACE

NOTES

"Money is a great tool, but a horrible master."
Sam Chesham

WEEKLY PLANNER

week of: _____

MONDAY

TUESDAY

WEDNESDAY

THURSDAY

FRIDAY

SATURDAY

SUNDAY

METAMORPHOSIS

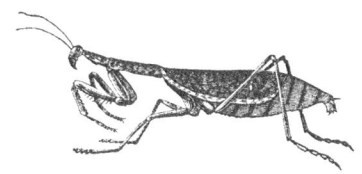

week of: _____

GRATITUDE

TRUTHS

OPPORTUNITIES FOR GROWTH

ENCOUNTERS AND FEELINGS

SELF CARE/SOUL CARE

LIES I NEED TO REPLACE

NOTES

"The season that you are in will pass. Your heart will heal.
The sun will come up, this too shall pass."
Rebecca Marklund

WEEKLY PLANNER

week of: _____

MONDAY

TUESDAY

WEDNESDAY

THURSDAY

FRIDAY

SATURDAY

SUNDAY

METAMORPHOSIS

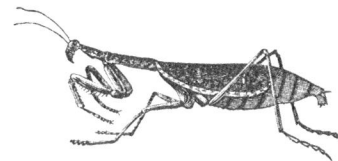

week of: _____

GRATITUDE

TRUTHS

OPPORTUNITIES FOR GROWTH

ENCOUNTERS AND FEELINGS

SELF CARE/SOUL CARE

LIES I NEED TO REPLACE

NOTES

"Rise warrior. It's time. Rise."
Unknown

NOTES AND REFLECTION

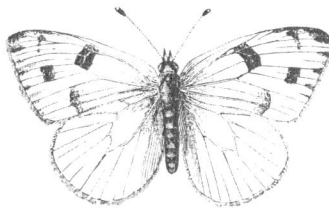

You've done a year of brave transformation. Some years may be more vigorous and transformative than others. Again, be gentle with yourself. Developing these habits of daily reflection is growth in itself, and everyones process is unique.

Take time to go back and reflect on the year, the events and journaling you've done. It's a healthy process to look back and see the changes and transformation and growth, it encourages us to continue on these life giving habits in years to come.

Keep up the wonderful hard work, of becoming the best version of yourself. You need that, your loved ones need that, your community needs that, and your world needs that as well.

Congratulations on the year behind, and all the best in the year ahead as you continue your process of metamorphosis.

Rebecca